WRITING FANTASY & SCIENCE FICTION

A TAKE-ACTION WORKBOOK

Saugeen Publishers
Kitchener, Ontario

Copyright © 2019 by Heather Wright.

All rights reserved. No part of this publication may be reproduced, distributed or transmitted in any form or by any means, including photocopying, recording, or other electronic or mechanical methods, without the prior written permission of the publisher, except in the case of brief quotations embodied in critical reviews and certain other noncommercial uses permitted by copyright law. For permission requests, write to the publisher, addressed "Attention: Permissions Coordinator," at the address below.

Heather Wright
hwrightwriter@gmail.com
http://www.wrightingwords.com

Book Layout ©2013 BookDesignTemplates.com
Cover image: ID 4144132 @ Pixabay

Writing Fantasy& Science Fiction: A Take-Action Workbook
Heather Wright
Saugeen Publishers
ISBN: 978-1-9991038-1-1

This book is dedicated to my husband and my son who introduced me to fantasy and science fiction. May they both live long and prosper.

I have to write because if I don't get something down then after a while. I feel it's going to bang the side of my head off.

    Terry Pratchett

The pen is mightier than the sword if the sword is very short, and the pen is very sharp.

    Terry Pratchett

Writing, to me, is simply thinking through my fingers.

    Isaac Asimov

Science fiction is any idea that occurs in the head and doesn't exist yet, but soon will, and will change everything for everybody, and nothing will ever be the same again. As soon as you have an idea that changes some small part of the world you are writing science fiction. It is always the art of the possible, never the impossible.

    Ray Bradbury

Contents

HOW TO USE THIS BOOK 1
CHARACTERS 5
RULES FOR MAGIC & SPECIAL POWERS 35
THE SCIENCE IN YOUR SCIENCE FICTION 41
PLOT PLANNERS 51
    CHAPTER-BY-CHAPTER 60
WORLD BUILDING 79
JOURNAL PAGES 95
CALENDAR 159
COLORING PAGES 184
ABOUT ME 195

HOW TO USE THIS BOOK

You are already doing your research, reading the fantastic books out there to help you write a great fantasy or science fiction novel. You have ideas, notes, reflections, information. **This book is your desk-top companion on your writing journey.**

Well-designed tools created especially for your genre will guide your creativity and keep you inspired. In this workbook, you can record details about your characters, your plot plans, your notes on world-building, and anything else you need to regularly refer to as you create your story. This workbook also includes journal pages where you can reflect on and celebrate your work plus a calendar to track your progress.

All your notes, thoughts, questions, planning—all in one place.

Inside this book you will find worksheets, planners, and journal pages to help you develop characters, find your story, and reflect on the process. Use this book to schedule your writing time, beat writer's block with a little coloring, and best of all, get the words on the page as you've been dreaming them.

You can find out more about all my books at your online bookseller or on my website: http://www.wrightingwords.com.

If you find this book of value, **please stop by your online bookseller and leave a review**. I appreciate your time and your honest comments. The series includes:

Characters

CHARACTERS

The following planners will help you learn more about your characters. I've added a notes page at the end of each one. As you work on your novel, you will discover more interesting things about your characters, and these pages give you a place to record those inspirations.

Writing speculative fiction gives you the opportunity to create characters in a wide variety of forms, and to give them skills that regular humans might not have. Since many fantasy and science fiction writers use the hero's journey template for plotting, you might also want to consider the following characters as part of story building:

Main Character (MC) – The person with whom the reader develops the closest relationship.

Mentor or Guide – helps MC with advice, wisdom, tools s/he will need on the journey.

Ally – the loyal friend who shares the journey and the danger.

Herald/Messenger – brings the message that will change the MC's life forever.

Trickster – adds fun to the story and sometimes trouble.

Shapeshifter- can appear to be trustworthy but can turn on the MC when needed most

Guardian- a character who must be defeated, passed, neutralized before the MC can continue with the journey.

Shadow (MC's opponent) – the villain in the piece, causing conflict and opposing the MC.

Not all these characters need appear, and some characters may encompass the traits of more than one of the above.

Main Character = MC

NOTES

Main Character's Name _____

Physical description	Social position, rank, special skills
Secret that character has told no one	One thing that character is afraid of
One thing/person that MC would do anything to protect	Attitude toward life, family, friends

Why MC is "chosen" for this task	Connection to ally/mentor/shadow
Something from the character's past that will help or hinder success	Internal conflict or insecurity that events in the story make worse or force character to overcome

NOTES

NOTES

Ally's Name _____

Physical description	Social position, rank, special skills
Secret that character has told no one	One thing that character is afraid of
One thing/person that character would do anything to protect	Attitude toward life, family, friends

Connection to MC or other key characters	Personality trait of sidekick that can cause trouble for MC

How ally's past can help or hinder the story	Internal conflict or insecurity that events in the story make worse or force character to overcome

NOTES

NOTES

Other Character _____

Physical description	Social position, rank, special skills
Secret that character has told no one	One thing that character is afraid of
One thing/person that character would do anything to protect	Attitude toward life, family, friends

Connection to MC	Connection to ally, mentor, shadow
How this character challenges the MC or helps progress	Character flaw / character strength

NOTES

NOTES

Other Character _____

Physical description	Social position, rank, special skills
Secret that character has told no one	One thing that character is afraid of
One thing/person that character would do anything to protect	Attitude toward life, family, friends

Connection to MC	Connection to ally, mentor, shadow
How this character challenges the MC or helps progress	Character flaw / character strength

NOTES

NOTES

Other Character _____

Physical description	Social position, rank, special skills
Secret that character has told no one	One thing that character is afraid of
One thing/person that character would do anything to protect	Attitude toward life, family, friends

Connection to MC	Connection to ally, mentor, shadow
How this character challenges the MC or helps progress	Character flaw / character strength

NOTES

NOTES

Other Character _____

Physical description	Social position, rank, special skills
Secret that character has told no one	One thing that character is afraid of
One thing/person that character would do anything to protect	Attitude toward life, family, friends

Connection to MC	Connection to ally, mentor, shadow
How this character challenges the MC or helps progress	Character flaw / character strength

NOTES

NOTES

NOTES

NOTES

Rules for Magic and Special Powers

RULES FOR MAGIC & SPECIAL POWERS

If you are going to grant your characters the use of magic or any other special abilities in your fantasy novel, it's worth spending some time working out how those powers will work in the world you create.

Here are some questions that you might want to answer to clarify your thoughts about the magic or special powers used by the characters in your book. Use the following pages to brainstorm your thoughts.

- Does everyone have access to special powers or skills, or are they restricted to only a select few?
- What are the rules of magic? Controls?
- Can magic backfire? Why?
- Are special circumstances, ingredients, locations required?
- Is there a cost to using magic?
- How are the select few trained, chosen, born?
- Who trains people in the use of magic?
- Does power increase or decrease with use, or is it unchanged?
- Can power be transferred?
- Are there good and bad powers, or is all power the same and derived from the same source?

NOTES

NOTES

NOTES

NOTES

The Science in Your Science Fiction

THE SCIENCE IN YOUR SCIENCE FICTION

As well as the other aspects of world-building that you need to consider, the role of science and technology in your story is key. If you get this wrong, you will lose readers. Science fiction readers know whether you've done your homework or simply watched too many Star Trek episodes.

Some of the things that your imagination thinks up may already be in the works somewhere. Margaret Atwood (*Handmaid's Tale, Oryx and Crake*) never used anything in her speculative fiction that wasn't already happening somewhere in the world now. Her research gave her the opportunity to use current science to capture the imagination of readers who were unaware that these things were possible today. Check recent science magazines to find out what is at the cutting edge of research now, and then speculate where it could go.

> *"I'm not a prophet. Let's get rid of that idea right now. Prophecies are really about now. In science fiction it's always about now. What else could it be about? There is no future. There are many possibilities, but we do not know which one we are going to have."*
>
> *Margaret Atwood*

- Does everyone have access to the technology or is it restricted to only a select few? How might the select few be trained, chosen, born?
- How does the technology/science affect day-to-day life? Housing? Lifestyle? Food? Entertainment? Religion?

Weapons? Defense? Clothing? Transportation? Fuel? International/interplanetary relations?
- Are the controls political, corporate, religious?
- How could this technology backfire? How is it vulnerable? Why might this happen? Are there factions opposing this technology?
- Are special circumstances, components, locations required? What resources are needed to maintain and run the technology? Are they limited or infinite?
- Is there a cost to using this technology? Environment? Human resources?
- Who trains people in the use of technology?
- What current technology could be expanded into this future: the use of graphene, Crispr, alternative energy sources, nanorobotics?
- Are there ethical dilemmas at the time of your story around the use of this technology?
- Were there initial ethical issues when the technology was introduced? How were these overcome?

NOTES

NOTES

NOTES

NOTES

NOTES

NOTES

NOTES

Plot Planners

[50]

PLOT PLANNERS

One of the standard plot lines for fantasy and science fiction novels is the hero's journey.

In 1949, a scholar named Joseph Campbell published a book called *The Hero with a Thousand Faces*. In the book, he explained what he had learned from studying religions, mythology and legends from around the world. He found one story that seemed to occur in all cultures, no matter when they existed in history or where they existed on the planet. This pattern for a story has become known as the "hero's journey" though, of course, the framework applies to stories about all genders.

The hero's journey pattern roughly follows the steps in the following list. Use the term "hero's journey" to search the Internet and you will find lots of examples and more detailed descriptions of the pattern. I'm sure as you read through the following list that you will recognize a book you've read or a movie you've watched that follows a similar pattern to the steps here.

- The hero has an "unusual" birth. Often the hero is an orphan or has something mysterious in his past.
- The hero is asked to do something that, at first, he doesn't want to do, so he says no. Then he is asked again, but this time he says yes.
- Early in the journey or to help make the decision above, the hero gets help from someone wise, a mentor
- The hero travels from the familiar world to the adventure world.

- The hero often has a helper or ally in the adventure world.
- The hero is tested many times by people and events.
- The hero faces a final battle where all could be won or lost.
- After the battle, the hero returns with something that benefits others

George Lucas used this pattern in his *Star Wars* films. Harry Potter and Katniss go on similar journeys. Not every part of your story must match the steps listed above, but the hero's journey is a plotting device that's worth thinking about when you tackle a big project like a novel.

Why have a plan at all? I always recommend creating an outline for your novel before you begin writing. Unless you have limitless time in which to write, an outline can be your friend. If you know what is going to happen next in your story, you can take advantage of short bursts of time to make progress on your novel.

If you type at 40 words per minute, you can write 600 words in 15 minutes—a good 2 pages! An outline also ensures that you will get some writing done on those days when the muse is on sick leave or sitting, sulking in the corner and refusing to come out and play.

You learned a lot about your characters in the previous pages. Now is the time to put that information to use as you send your main character (MC) on his or her journey.

WORKSHEET FOR HERO'S JOURNEY STORY PLANNING

Working Title of Story: _____

The main character is: _____

MC has a mysterious background	
MC has a mentor or guide	
MC is offered a challenge but refuses	
MC accepts the challenge	
MC has an ally	

MC fights many battles	

MC has moment of black despair	
MC faces one last "life or death" battle	
MC returns with a prize for him/herself or for the community	

NOTES

NOTES

NOTES

NOTES

CHAPTER-BY-CHAPTER

Here's a chapter-by-chapter breakdown of the journey template. Of course, your novel may be a lot longer than this, so there are extra pages at the end to create further plot notes.

Chapters 1 and 2

Introduction of your main character and the world in which he or she lives.

MC is challenged with an adventure that will lead from comfort of current world.

Chapter 3

MC accepts challenge and prepares to leave. Ally and Mentor may take on a larger role here.

Chapters 4 through 9

MC travels in the strange world encountering many challenges and fighting many battles. Both inner and outer conflicts are at play here.

Chapter 10

MC faces black despair doubting his or her ability to succeed.

Chapters 11

MC engages in one final life or death battle.

Chapter 12

MC is victorious and returns with a prize for self or community.

World Building

WORLD BUILDING

Use the next pages to brainstorm the various components of the world you are creating for your story. List the questions you need to research, write down any resources, or draw any maps or illustrations of clothing, homes, jewelry, etc. that you may need for reference.

Here are the topics listed on the following pages to help you build the world for your novel:

- Government/ruling class
- Money/how the economy works
- Religious class and power
- Geography
- Climate
- Clothing and how produced/purchased
- Food/diet
- Transportation
- Measures of time and distance
- Communication – letters/telepathy/messengers—in SF consider communication over long distances. Ursula le Guin invented the Ansible to communicate over large distances in real time.
- Housing
- Science/Technology
- School/training
- Wild life/vegetation
- Medicine
- Astronomy
- Non-humans

Government/ruling class

Money/how the economy works-

Religious class and powers

Geography

Climate

Clothing/how produced/made

Food/diet

Transportation

Measures of time & distance

Communication

Housing/fuel

Science/Technology

School/training

Wild life/vegetation

Medicine

Astronomy

Non-Humans

NOTES

NOTES

Maps and Sketches

Maps and Sketches

Maps and Sketches

Journal Pages

JOURNAL PAGES

Here are 30 days of journal pages for you to record your progress through this book and through the beginnings of drafting your novel. Completing these pages will help you reflect on your process, determine next steps, and record any shiny, do-not-belong-in-this-novel ideas that come to you while you're working on your current project.

When things get tough, or you feel you are blocked, it's easy to want to drop what you are doing and go with the next shiny thing in your mind. I encourage you to capture these ideas but leave them for later.

Yes, there are writing days when you feel as if you're trying to run uphill in two feet of mud, but those feelings are also part of the writer's life. Every project will encounter them. Every writer faces them—and you are a writer, and you will overcome them.

Finishing is your best reward.

Date _____

The Step I Took Toward My Goal

My Surprises, Inspirations, Shiny Things

My Next Steps

To Do (research, word count goals, reading the experts ....)

Date _____

The Step I Took Toward My Goal

My Surprises, Inspirations, Shiny Things

My Next Steps

To Do (research, word count goals, reading the experts ....)

Date _____

The Step I Took Toward My Goal

___

My Surprises, Inspirations, Shiny Things

My Next Steps

To Do (research, word count goals, reading the experts ....)

Date _____

The Step I Took Toward My Goal

My Surprises, Inspirations, Shiny Things

My Next Steps

To Do (research, word count goals, reading the experts ....)

Date _____

The Step I Took Toward My Goal

_____
_____
_____
_____
_____
_____
_____

My Surprises, Inspirations, Shiny Things

_____
_____
_____
_____
_____
_____
_____

My Next Steps

To Do (research, word count goals, reading the experts ....)

Date _____

The Step I Took Toward My Goal

My Surprises, Inspirations, Shiny Things

My Next Steps

To Do (research, word count goals, reading the experts ….)

Date _____

The Step I Took Toward My Goal

My Surprises, Inspirations, Shiny Things

My Next Steps

To Do (research, word count goals, reading the experts ....)

Date _____

The Step I Took Toward My Goal

My Surprises, Inspirations, Shiny Things

My Next Steps

To Do (research, word count goals, reading the experts ....)

Date _____

The Step I Took Toward My Goal

My Surprises, Inspirations, Shiny Things

My Next Steps

To Do (research, word count goals, reading the experts ....)

Date _____

The Step I Took Toward My Goal

My Surprises, Inspirations, Shiny Things

My Next Steps

To Do (research, word count goals, reading the experts ….)

Date _____

The Step I Took Toward My Goal

My Surprises, Inspirations, Shiny Things

My Next Steps

To Do (research, word count goals, reading the experts ….)

Date _____

The Step I Took Toward My Goal

My Surprises, Inspirations, Shiny Things

My Next Steps

To Do (research, word count goals, reading the experts ....)

Date _____

The Step I Took Toward My Goal

My Surprises, Inspirations, Shiny Things

My Next Steps

To Do (research, word count goals, reading the experts ….)

Date _____

The Step I Took Toward My Goal

My Surprises, Inspirations, Shiny Things

My Next Steps

To Do (research, word count goals, reading the experts ....)

Date _____

The Step I Took Toward My Goal

_____

_____

_____

_____

_____

_____

My Surprises, Inspirations, Shiny Things

_____

_____

_____

_____

_____

_____

My Next Steps

To Do (research, word count goals, reading the experts ....)

Date _____

The Step I Took Toward My Goal

My Surprises, Inspirations, Shiny Things

My Next Steps

To Do (research, word count goals, reading the experts ....)

Date _____

The Step I Took Toward My Goal

My Surprises, Inspirations, Shiny Things

My Next Steps

To Do (research, word count goals, reading the experts ....)

Date _____

The Step I Took Toward My Goal

My Surprises, Inspirations, Shiny Things

My Next Steps

To Do (research, word count goals, reading the experts ....)

Date _____

The Step I Took Toward My Goal

My Surprises, Inspirations, Shiny Things

My Next Steps

To Do (research, word count goals, reading the experts ....)

Date _____

The Step I Took Toward My Goal

My Surprises, Inspirations, Shiny Things

My Next Steps

To Do (research, word count goals, reading the experts ….)

Date _____

The Step I Took Toward My Goal

My Surprises, Inspirations, Shiny Things

My Next Steps

To Do (research, word count goals, reading the experts ….)

Date _____

The Step I Took Toward My Goal

My Surprises, Inspirations, Shiny Things

My Next Steps

To Do (research, word count goals, reading the experts ....)

Date _____

The Step I Took Toward My Goal

My Surprises, Inspirations, Shiny Things

My Next Steps

To Do (research, word count goals, reading the experts ....)

Date _____

The Step I Took Toward My Goal

_____
_____
_____
_____
_____
_____

My Surprises, Inspirations, Shiny Things

_____
_____
_____
_____
_____
_____

My Next Steps

To Do (research, word count goals, reading the experts ....)

Date _____

The Step I Took Toward My Goal

My Surprises, Inspirations, Shiny Things

My Next Steps

To Do (research, word count goals, reading the experts ....)

Date _____

The Step I Took Toward My Goal

My Surprises, Inspirations, Shiny Things

My Next Steps

To Do (research, word count goals, reading the experts ….)

Date _____

The Step I Took Toward My Goal

My Surprises, Inspirations, Shiny Things

My Next Steps

To Do (research, word count goals, reading the experts ….)

Date _____

The Step I Took Toward My Goal

My Surprises, Inspirations, Shiny Things

My Next Steps

To Do (research, word count goals, reading the experts ....)

Date _____

The Step I Took Toward My Goal

My Surprises, Inspirations, Shiny Things

My Next Steps

To Do (research, word count goals, reading the experts ....)

Date _____

The Step I Took Toward My Goal

My Surprises, Inspirations, Shiny Things

My Next Steps

To Do (research, word count goals, reading the experts ….)

Date _____

The Step I Took Toward My Goal

My Surprises, Inspirations, Shiny Things

My Next Steps

To Do (research, word count goals, reading the experts ....)

Calendar

CALENDAR

It can take a long time to write a book, so I've included a full year of blank calendars for you to use to track your progress. Since this book contains a collection of your thoughts and plans, it's a good place to record your word count or time spent writing or whatever you choose to log to keep you inspired by your progress.

Remember, writing in small pieces works, and you have the advantage of having spent time outlining your story. You don't have to wait for the muse to drop by; you know what you are working on next. And you can write out of order, too, if you like. If one scene is really clear in your mind, write it, and put it where it belongs later.

Consider the numbers. If you write 250 words (1 page double-spaced) for 300 days a year you will have 75,000 words. Even if you only type at 30 words a minute, 250 words takes less than 10 minutes a day. I find these numbers encouraging—and they also take away the excuse that I don't have enough time to write.

NOTES

Month _____

Sun	Mon	Tues	Wed	Thurs	Fri	Sat

NOTES

Month _____

Sun	Mon	Tues	Wed	Thurs	Fri	Sat

NOTES

Month _____

Sun	Mon	Tues	Wed	Thurs	Fri	Sat

NOTES

Month _____

Sun	Mon	Tues	Wed	Thurs	Fri	Sat

NOTES

Month _____

Sun	Mon	Tues	Wed	Thurs	Fri	Sat

NOTES

Month _____

Sun	Mon	Tues	Wed	Thurs	Fri	Sat

NOTES

Month _____

Sun	Mon	Tues	Wed	Thurs	Fri	Sat

NOTES

Month _____

Sun	Mon	Tues	Wed	Thurs	Fri	Sat

NOTES

Month _____

Sun	Mon	Tues	Wed	Thurs	Fri	Sat

NOTES

Month _____

Sun	Mon	Tues	Wed	Thurs	Fri	Sat

NOTES

Month _____

Sun	Mon	Tues	Wed	Thurs	Fri	Sat

NOTES

Month _____

Sun	Mon	Tues	Wed	Thurs	Fri	Sat

Coloring Pages

Image by KaylinArt on Pixabay

Image by KaylinArt on Pixabay

ABOUT ME

I always have more than one work-in-progress. I own too many journals, and I love red licorice, buttered popcorn, and chocolate–not together. I'm grateful for coffee shops where I can go to kickstart stalled projects. I love music, old films, and sing soprano in a choir. (Secret: I leave the Bs for those who can land them without a squeak.)

I can't imagine my life without writers, watching them become motivated and empowered, and reading the great work that they create. As a coach, I love working one-on-one with writers of all ages. My current clients range in age from 15 to 90.

I am also a freelance writer, writing about everything from orchids to wind turbines to weddings to PVC pipe. I have written for national and local publications, and for educational publishers and industry.

My website, **http://www.wrightingwords.com**, hosts my blog and offers links to all my books for writers. You'll also find lots of free resources for writers of all ages and their teachers, too.

If you found this book of value, **please stop by your online bookseller and leave a review**. I appreciate your time and your honest comments.

www.ingramcontent.com/pod-product-compliance
Lightning Source LLC
Chambersburg PA
CBHW081356070526
44583CB00020B/2570